Faith, Hope, and Love

The Emil Brunner Library

Christianity and Civilisation
Dogmatics (In Three Volumes)
The Divine Imperative: A Study in Christian Ethics
Eternal Hope
Faith, Hope and Love
The Great Invitation: Zürich Sermons
I Believe in the Living God: Sermons on the Apostles Creed
Justice and Social Order
The Letter to the Romans
Man in Revolt: A Christian Anthropology
The Mediator: A Study of the Central Doctrine of the Christian Faith
The Misunderstanding of the Church

Faith, Hope and Love

Emil Brunner

James Clarke & Co

James Clarke & Co.

P.O. Box 60
Cambridge
CB1 2NT
United Kingdom

www.jamesclarke.co
publishing@jamesclarke.co

Paperback ISBN: 978 0 227 17919 2
PDF ISBN: 978 0 227 17921 5
ePub ISBN: 978 0 227 17920 8

British Library Cataloguing in Publication Data
A record is available from the British Library

First published by the Westminster Press, Philadelphia 1956.
First British edition published by The Lutterworth Press 1957.
This edition published 2023

Copyright © Emil Brunner, 1956

All rights reserved. No part of this edition may be reproduced,
stored electronically or in any retrieval system, or transmitted
in any form or by any means, electronic, mechanical,
photocopying, recording, or otherwise, without
prior written permission from the Publisher
(permissions@jamesclarke.co).

Contents

Foreword   vii

Introduction: Faith, Hope, and Love as Problems of Theology   1

   Faith   5

   Hope   22

   Love   44

Foreword

These three addresses were delivered as the Earl Lectures at Berkeley, California, in the spring of 1955. The theme which, surprisingly enough, had never to my knowledge been treated in a systematic monograph, aroused so much interest that, contrary to my intention but in response to numerous requests, I decided to publish them. Perhaps it was the particular theological method that appeared novel to those who heard the lectures. This method is marked by a consistently existential exposition of the Biblical Word, in which indeed the Word is to be understood not so much in the Bultmann-Heidegger connotation as in that of Kierkegaard. Readers will find that by this method new insight into the meaning, the unity, and the difference of the three concepts will be gained.

My friend Professor Hugh Vernon White has prepared the lectures for publication by ironing out the most obvious evidences of my imperfect mastery of the English language. I express to him my heartfelt thanks for this unselfish and painstaking service. My thanks are due also to Dr. Stuart LeRoy Anderson, president of Pacific School of Religion, and the Earl Committee, whose hospitality my wife and I enjoyed for an unforgettable week.

Emil Brunner

Introduction:
Faith, Hope, and Love
as Problems of Theology

Faith, hope, and love are facts of every Christian's experience. Why should one wish to make theological problems of them? Such a question might be expected to arise in the mind of the layman. And just because the three are such common and popular pulpit themes, the theologian might ask with equal justification why a theologian should choose them as subjects for a series of lectures. Standing between these two fires as, in the main, I do; being consciously a lay theologian; never forgetting that the vast majority of Christians are not theologians, and having also observed, again and again, that the questions that worry the layman are both more interesting and more difficult than those which are the favored subjects of discussion by theologians, I have chosen a theme that is certainly close to the interest of laymen and also difficult enough and even new enough, for the theologian.

Although these three words are in common use, not only among Christians, but in the general vocabulary, and although the triad constitutes a popular series for sermons, it is a fact and a strange fact that, at least so far as my knowledge goes, it has never been made the subject of thorough theological study. Why, in the New Testament, are these three words related in such a close and conspicuous unity? What is the connection of the three concepts – faith, hope, and love – each of which is, in its own right, one of the main words of the Christian message? As long as we do not know why these words have thus been brought together, we do not really know what each of them means and what its importance is in the Christian life. This, then, is the theological problem that I propose to deal with in these three lectures.

The strange thing about faith, hope, and love is that in Christian doctrinal thought they constitute, so to speak, rivals, in so far as each one of them could claim to be the most important. Even more, each of them expresses the whole of Christian existence, the totality of what it means to be a Christian. Each of them is, not merely one, but *the* criterion of true Christianity. They are not, as Roman Catholic doctrine declares, the three supreme virtues; they are not virtues at all, as we shall see later. Nor is their "threeness" a mere sum, so that one can be added to the other. Each one expresses the totality of Christian existence. How is this possible?

This problem was to me a subject of worry for many years; until I discovered that the threefold totality is related to a basic fact of man's existence as

Introduction

a human being – every man's existence is in the three dimensions of time. He lives in the past, in the future, and in the present. We live in the past – by memory. Without having our past with us, without remembering both our individual history and the history of man or mankind, we should not be *human;* we should be animals only. Man is the historic being, the being that has his past with him.

But we live also in the future – by expectation, hoping, fearing, planning. Without anticipating our future we should not be human either. It is as well the foreseeing of what we might, could, and should be that distinguishes us from the animals. We live, of course, in the present, but for the most part we are not aware of the fact that this "being in the present" is most problematic. I wish I could say that I do live in the present; that is indeed my highest ideal. Somehow it must be true that we do live in the present; otherwise we should not live at all.

Since this is true of human life as such – that we live in the past, in the future, and in the present – we must now ask how we, as Christians, live in the past, in the future, and in the present, and that means how our relation to Jesus Christ affects our living in the past, the future, and the present. The answer of the New Testament is precisely these three words: we live in the past by faith; we live in the future by hope; we live in the present by love. That is the reason why each one of these three great words expresses the whole of our existence without competing with the others. If Saint Paul says, "Love is the greatest of these," this does not mean a difference of greater or lesser importance. All are equally essential and total, because each expresses the relation to Jesus in a particular dimension of time.

Faith

We start our analysis of faith by a simple statement of fact. While it is obvious to every reader of the New Testament that faith is supreme in the life of the Christian, this is not true in the profession of other forms of religion. We cannot properly call these other religions "faiths." *Mystical* religion, for example, does not speak of faith but of the experience of oneness or becoming one with the Infinite. Neither does *primitive* religion speak of faith; it lives by the encounter with numinous things, events and forces. *Speculative,* philosophical religion, again, does not speak of faith but of knowledge of the Divine. These three types of religion have one common denominator: they have no relation to history; they are non-historical or ahistorical.

In Christianity, however, relation to a historical event is dominant. We are Christians because we are related to a historical fact, that fact of history which we all know, the person of Jesus Christ in whom God has revealed himself and by whom man's situation is changed from one of being lost to one of being redeemed. The gospel of Christ witnesses to this fact as being absolutely decisive for man, and that through his faith. This fact not only is unique; it is explicitly spoken of as unique. It is not unique by comparison, because it is above comparison. It is unique by its very nature as unprecedented and unrepeatable. Redemption or reconciliation either has never happened or it has happened once for all.

The prologue to the Fourth Gospel has stated this fact and given the formula of its uniqueness in the concept which has become basic for all Christian theology: the Word has become flesh. By this formula it is not denied but, on the contrary, affirmed that God has revealed himself and his Word before the coming of Jesus Christ. This was, of course, through the prophetic Word. What marks the revelation through Jesus Christ is that this Word has now become flesh, creaturely life or, in common terminology, historical person. And the same author, John, in his First Epistle, accentuates this historical factuality by writing: "That which we have heard, that which we have seen with our eyes, that which we have beheld, that which we have touched with our hands." You see, four times he asserts the historical factuality. In terms of our own thought we might say that the eternal Word has incorporated itself, become a fact in historical time.

The witnesses to this fact are the apostles. As we have just heard from John, they are eyewitnesses;

that is, they can testify that this fact is a fact in history, in the order of reality that we grasp with our natural organs of perception. "We have seen, we have heard, we have touched with our hands" – this is one side of the event: On the other hand, the real significance, the divine Word in this flesh, is not something that can be grasped with our senses. That Jesus is the Christ "is not," as Jesus says to Peter, "revealed by flesh and blood but by my Father who is in heaven." This two-sidedness of the fact is that which was later formulated in the doctrine of the "two natures" of Christ. He is a man like us, but at the same time he is Immanuel, which means "God with us." "God was in Christ this is the mystery of the person of Jesus Christ, the God-man, truly man, truly God.

Now we must ask, Why is this so all-important? What difference does it make to me whether this is so, or not? The apostles answer this question by speaking of the work of Jesus Christ. They speak of his work in such terms as "revelation," "redemption," "salvation," and thus they explain the change in the condition of man which is brought about by Jesus Christ, seen or apprehended by faith. What this faith is we shall see later. First we have to make clear what the fact is to which this faith is related; more precisely, what this fact means to faith and why it is so essential that this fact be seen as unique, *once for all.*

Turn again to the prologue of Saint John's Gospel; he uses such words as life, light, grace, and truth. Man's situation is such that he does not know God, that he is devoid of truth, that therefore he is in darkness and separated from God, the true Life. With his own reason he may form certain ideas of God through philosophical or metaphysical speculation. But this does not help him much – although it is not quite without significance – because the God that man *thinks* is not the God who himself speaks and acts, not the God who opens his heart and reveals his purpose, not the God of love, not the God who is Love. But it is just this that matters, because to know the God who is Love – the God who loves us sinful, rebellious men in spite of what we are – this is precisely the good news; this is the turning point in man's history.

The New Testament uses the word "redemption" to mark this change, and it points particularly to the cross of Christ as the point at which this change takes place. It is not, as has often been asserted, Saint Paul only who stresses this; we find the same emphasis in the writings of John, in Hebrews, in the epistles of Peter, and in the Synoptic Gospels, where the story of the Passion of Jesus is related with more detail than any other event. But again it is never a so-called objective fact that is indicated. It is always that fact of history as seen with the eyes of faith; just that and nothing else. The cross of Christ is the point where God's love meets sinful man, if the sinful man, also, stands there, that is, by faith. God's act is always an act that engages man and has meaning only if man lets himself be engaged, or be touched. God's act in Christ is that he gives man a new "standing" and thereby creates for him a new situation. In the cross of Christ, God says to man: "There is where you ought to be. Jesus, my Son, hangs there in your stead; his tragedy is the tragedy of your life. You are the rebel who should be hanged on the gallows. But, lo, I suffer instead of you and because of you, because I love you in spite of what you are. My love for you is so great that I meet you there with my love, there on the cross. I cannot meet you anywhere else. You must meet me there, by identifying yourself with the one on the cross. It is by this identification that I, God, can meet you, man, in him, saying to you what I say to him: 'My beloved son.'"

The cross of Christ on Golgotha is a historic fact just as truly as the murder of Julius Caesar in Rome. But the murder of Caesar has no importance for us. We do not meet God there; much less do we meet there the love of God by which he loves us in spite of ourselves. What makes *this* historical fact all-important is that God meets us at the cross and nowhere else. If it is really true that there we meet God, in his incredible love for us in spite of what we are – and faith knows that this is so – then this fact is of unique importance. It means that God, mystery in himself, has removed the veil and revealed his heart to man, has changed man's condition entirely, from that of a godless rebel to that of a beloved son.

The historian would say: Yes, the crucifixion of Jesus is a unique fact; it took place then and there and nowhere else. But he would add, as a historian: But the uniqueness is relative; there are many similar occurrences recorded, such as the death of Socrates and the martyrs. For the believer, however, this uniqueness is not relative but absolute, because nowhere else in history has God revealed himself in the cross of his Son. It is absolutely unique because only there has that change in the situation of man taken place that is not merely *a* change but *the* change, which we call "redemption" or "reconciliation." It is a fact that has occurred once and for all, for this redeeming revelation, this reconciliation – if it is really that – cannot take place more than once. If God really has reconciled the world to himself in Christ, he does not do it again. He has done it, for all time. God *has* reconciled the world to himself for good, forever.

So it is indeed a unique fact in a way that is not merely historical. This historic fact is unique in a sense that transcends the plane of history. In its eternity has entered time, the time world, or temporality; it is God himself who has entered history. It is *so* that the New Testament understands this fact. And to this fact faith is related; in this fact faith finds it content or object.

More than that it is a relation to this fact in which faith consists. I mean, of course, the Christian faith. As we have already seen, there is no such historic fact in any other religion. There is a sort of historical reference in the Mohammedan faith – for example, the historic fact of the Hegira, Mohammed's flight from Mecca to Medina. But no Moslem would claim that this is the fact of redemption, and so of absolute importance to his faith. He does not even claim that the life of Mohammed has such an importance. For the Jews too, the Exodus of the people of Israel is an important fact, but no Jew would claim that this exodus of the people from Egypt is redemption for him. It is precisely such a claim, however, that the New Testament makes as to the content of the Christian faith.

* * *

So much for the fact itself, the historic fact in its uniqueness, its once-for-all character. Now let us turn to faith itself, faith as an act of the heart. So far we have used a very indefinite, vague word, namely, the "relation" to this fact. We must now be more precise in describing this "relation," this faith. If faith is so strictly and completely bound to this historic fact or event, Jesus Christ, the question inevitably arises whether this does not bring faith into the sphere of historical relativity and uncertainty. Do we know whether what the Gospels tell us about Jesus Christ is really true? This question has become particularly urgent, it seems, through the critical study of the New Testament as source of our knowledge. What are the true facts of the life of Jesus? Our knowledge of Jesus seems to be so uncertain. How can absolute certainty, the certainty of faith, be united with uncertainty as to fact? The most recent school of New Testament research, the so-called *Formgeschichte,* has shown us that much of the New Testament narrative does not give us a historic picture but the figure of Jesus as the Early Church saw it and words which the early Christians put into his mouth. However, from this same school has also come a new insight which may give us the solution to our problem. The quest for the so-called "historic Jesus" as the object of secular historic research indeed leads us to uncertainty. But is this quest important for us as believers? The so-called "historic Jesus" is a picture that is produced by a secular objectivity which as such is of no interest whatever to faith. Faith has nothing to do with this so-called "historic Jesus" but with Jesus the Christ, Jesus witnessed to by his apostles as being the Christ. God's revelation in Christ is not a historic fact in the secular sense; rather, it is the reality of Jesus seen through the open eyes of faith, Jesus witnessed to as the Christ, the Son of God. Accordingly, the distinction between the so-called "historic Jesus" and the Jesus of *Gemeindetheologie* is irrelevant for faith. Faith is based on the witness of the apostles about Jesus the Christ.

Let us make this clear by comparing the Synoptic Gospels with that of Saint John. There *is* a great difference indeed. But this difference is not of such nature as to be of interest to the Christian. It may be that the Synoptics are closer to the so-called "objective facts" of Jesus' life in which a neutral historian would be interested. However, on their side, the

Synoptics are not biographers; they are not interested in the biography of Jesus, but in witnessing to Jesus as the Christ, just as John is. And John is a witness of Christ who wants to let us see nobody else but the *Jesus of history* as seen by the eyes of faith. Therefore the intention of both and the witness of both is the same. While the Synoptics may come closer to the objective facts, John, in his turn, may be closer to the faith, to the meaning of the facts of the life and person of Jesus the Christ. Their narrative about the crucifixion of Jesus may be different in details, as indeed they are, but there is not the slightest doubt that they are speaking of the same event, the crucifixion on Golgotha. And they are both speaking of the event with such great interest because for both this is the decisive thing, the act of God's revelation and redemption. Thus the whole heated debate of a hundred years of scholarly work is, after all, almost completely beside the point so far as faith is concerned. *That* historic fact which is of decisive interest for faith, Jesus the Christ crucified under Pontius Pilate, is beyond any historic doubt. That fact is included in all apostolic witness about Jesus the Christ, and *this* is the fact in which we believe.

The second point that I want to emphasize is closely related to this first one, namely, that faith is not related to history in the sense of objective facts as such. Such an objectivism is not in the nature of true faith. The revelation of God and redemption through Jesus Christ are not facts of history. This very making of a distinction between objectivity and subjectivity fails to do justice to what both revelation and redemption mean. God himself speaking to us through the life and death of Jesus is not history in the usual sense of the word. Where God speaks to us there is the end of history; there is an encounter of God with us in which we are ourselves engaged. It is a fact of history laden with eternal, trans-historical reality and meaning, and this reality is grasped only by the act of faith. We can grasp Jesus as the Christ, the Son of God, the only Saviour, only if our hearts are opened for him and by him. The meaning of his death on the cross can be seen and understood only if we ourselves are identified with that death, and this is exactly what faith in the cross means. To make the nature of encounter clear and the distinction between objective and subjective obsolete as something irrelevant, I will use an analogy – a strange analogy, you may say: A reporter goes to Korea to provide the people at home in America with a true picture of what is happening in the Korean war. If he wants to be objective, merely objective, he will go to the headquarters and collect all the factual material assembled there. But if he does that he will not be a good reporter. The good war reporter goes into the front lines. He exposes himself to the shells of the enemy. He shares the life of the soldier. Then he can give a true picture of what happens in the Korean war. Now this is what happens with the cross of Jesus Christ and you. You can't understand the cross of Christ without going there into the front line where God meets you. It cannot be understood objectively from the safe distance of objectivity. And this analogy which I have used is almost word for word the one used by the apostles themselves. They say that in order to understand Jesus Christ crucified you have to be crucified yourself. You have to die with Christ on the cross. You remember Paul's words, "I am crucified with Christ"? It is only so that you can know what the cross *is* and means. In describing this identification with Jesus Christ, Paul uses the language of the Greek mystics; at the same time he also uses the contrasting language of the Jewish courts – justification, reconciliation, forgiveness.

I said in the beginning of this lecture that mystics do not speak of faith but of experience. Primitive religion does not speak of faith but of encounter with numinous things and events. Philosophical religion does not speak of faith but of knowledge. In the description that the New Testament gives of faith we have all three of these. Yes, indeed, faith is mystical experience, namely, becoming one with Christ. Indeed it is an encounter with the numinous, the supernatural, being an encounter with the living God. Yes, indeed, it is knowledge, recognition of the mystery of God revealed in Christ. And because faith is *all* that, it is none of them; it is not mystical religion, it is not primitive religion, it is not philosophical religion. The mystic does not know of reconciliation or of forgiveness of guilt. The primitive does not know the real holy or the real numinous, namely, the holy God who gives himself in love. Philosophical gnosis does not know of that knowledge which consists in *being* known, that knowledge which is no more mastering something, but which consists in being mastered.

We should take particular account of the close connection between faith and God's love. If faith is understood as belief in something, some doctrine, some creed, or some fact, it is, in itself, the same act of "believing it." Faith, however, in the New Testament sense, *pistis,* is an act of an entirely personal nature determined by "He" or "Thou," belonging to the dimension of I-Thou, not I-It. Its closest analogy in our daily experience is found in entrusting oneself to someone. To entrust oneself to another means to abandon the mastery of oneself, to give oneself to the other. Now, in ordinary human relations this is never quite possible; complete self-abandonment, if it should really happen, would be irresponsibility. We cannot and should not entrust ourselves to anyone completely, because no one can command our complete confidence. No human person is absolutely trustworthy, because every human person is a frail being, after all, and therefore might fail us; he is a sinful being motivated by self-love and therefore might fail us. Moreover, he cannot take responsibility for us; *we* are and remain responsible for ourselves. We cannot and should not entrust ourselves to any human being. But it is different with God, who is all-powerful and whose nature is love. God alone is absolutely trustworthy, not being frail but all powerful, not being selfish but love itself. It is that God whose infinite love is revealed in Jesus Christ who makes it possible for us to entrust ourselves completely and without reserve, because he has revealed himself without reserve as unconditioned love. It is to him and only to him, who is holy Love as revealed in the cross of Christ, that we *can,* that we *dare* to give ourselves completely. In doing so we do not lose our responsibility as we should if we entrusted ourselves completely to a human being. On the contrary, we become fully responsible only in entrusting ourselves to God. Love is the fulfillment of human responsibility. For he that loveth his neighbor hath fulfilled "the law." "Love is the fulfillment of the law," and therefore of responsibility.

This consideration gives us a new understanding of what the cross of Christ means. We say, "Man is forgiven his sin." Yes, indeed! But we do not mean just forgiveness. If we speak simply of forgiveness, our moral sense is not satisfied. It represents a too easy brushing aside of moral responsibility for our guilt. Can our guilt be just annihilated? Is there not in it an ultimate reality? Yes, indeed, says the cross of Christ. Your guilt is an ultimate reality insomuch that not even the love of God can simply pass it by. The suffering which you feel that your guilt ought to inflict upon you has been supremely suffered by

Him in whom God gives you forgiveness and love. God takes your guilt so seriously that he takes it upon himself. Christ sacrifices himself in order to reach you with God's love. The cross is therefore a manifestation of both God's holiness or justice and God's love. It makes manifest the reality of guilt at the same time as it makes manifest the unconditional love of God, his love-in-spite-of-us.

We shall understand this most important point best if we come back to the question that was raised in the beginning of this lecture: In what sense is faith our relation to the past? We have answered this question already in so far as we have shown the relation of faith to a fact of the past, namely, to the cross of Christ. But now we have to see also the relation of faith to our own past, our own history. This is exactly what the cross is and means. Christ has taken upon himself our guilt. What is guilt? Our guilt is nothing but our past as it appears in the light of the holy God. We know that we are sinners. We might think that we can get rid of our sin by a change of heart. But even if we should have a change of heart, that would not affect our past sin. And that is what guilt means – our past sin. This past sin is our guilt. We cannot do anything about our guilt because we cannot do anything about our past. It has gone out of our hands by becoming past. Well, modern man has a way of dealing with his past; he forgets it. But that is no solution. Modern man forgets about his past and by so doing he loses a whole dimension of his existence. To use a term from bookkeeping, we have to "carry" our past, we have to carry it over into the present. That is the most human act of our life – recognizing our guilt as a reality of our present.

And this is exactly what God does. He does not say to our guilty hearts, "Forget about it." He takes our life as a whole and he wants us to take our past seriously. We *are* now guilty for the past. We have to give account of our past to him, the Judge, who knows it. If we forget about it, he does not. If we do not take it seriously, he does. Still, even if we remember our past as guilt, we cannot do anything about it. If I may speak again in the terms of business, the mortgage is not in our hands; it is in God's hands. We cannot forgive ourselves; forgiveness is *his* prerogative. He *does* forgive, but he does it so that it becomes clear to us how seriously he takes our guilt. It costs him nothing less than the life of his Son. In reaching out to us he has to wade, so to speak, through our guilt. He wants to show his love for us. He shows it at the same time that he shows us our guilt; that is the cross of Christ. He suffers instead of us. It is therefore in facing the cross that we become fully aware of the seriousness of our guilt, of the importance of our guilty past. The cross of Christ is a fact of world history; it is also a fact of our personal history, for it is for me as well as for mankind that Jesus Christ suffers. It is for the world as well as for me that Christ has died. It is to mankind as well as to me that God declares his unconditioned love: "God so loved the world."

It is then and there that the gates of heaven are opened and the gates of hell closed. He, Christ crucified, is the door to the Father's house. No one can come to the Father but through him, through this door. No one knows how great, how incomprehensible and unconditional, God's love is but the one who sees, by faith, God taking upon himself the burden of our past in order to show how much he loves us. God annuls our past in order to free us from the burden of our past and to give us true presence in his love. With this our third lecture will deal.

Our description of faith, however, would not be complete if we did not point to the necessary connection between faith and hope. God makes us his children, his adopted children, through Christ, and his children we *are,* now. By faith in his love, his love-in-spite-of-us, our existence is changed because we are no more sinners; we are now his beloved children through Christ. Man through Christ gets back, and gets back more fully, what he is created by God to be, His image. This image, effaced by sin, is recreated, and as re-created it is more than what it was by creation. We *are* now, through Christ, sons of God, and we are what we are by his love. By faith we receive his love as a new existence.

But the question arises, Is that really true? Are we really living in the love of God so that we reflect the rays of his light in our lives? Yes and no. Yes, by faith, really. No, because it is only by faith that this is so and not yet by sight. Our new life is, as yet, hidden in Christ, as the apostle says; therefore it is not yet a visible reality to be grasped by everyone, or at least not yet an unambiguously visible reality. It is a "treasure in an earthen vessel," or, to use another figure, a heavenly light in a very dim lantern. We *are* heirs of eternal life because the love of God is eternal, for eternity. But we must die. As long as we live in this body of death, the eternal life, our heritage, is merely assured; it is not "paid out" heritage. We therefore expect the realization of this promise, the cash value, so to speak, of the testament which is signed by God with the blood of Christ, his Son. This is what we hope, what we expect in the future. But the certainty of it *is* present, in the love of Christ from which nothing can separate us, not even death. So, in faith as the receptacle of God's love, in that past which faith grasps, our present and our future are contained.

Hope

Hope is another basic word found in everyone's vocabulary. No one can live without having some hope. But what *is* hope? If we take the word in its most general sense, it means anticipation of the future. By hope man lives in the future, and this, as we have already said, belongs to the character of life as human. A man who did not live in the future would not be human. Hope, however, is only one of the modes of anticipating the future. There is also fear; there is anxiety, and there are provision and planning. Hope, fear, and anxiety are the passive forms of the expectation of coming things, of the expectation of either good or bad things to come or of uncertainty about the character of what is to come. Planning, however, is the active form implying man's control of his future.

Our question is, What is the basis of hope, that is, of the expectation of good things to come? Of course hope, as the opposite of fear and anxiety, must be based on some knowledge of facts which, as we say, "give hope." We do not now consider the innumerable things for which man can hope, from good weather for tomorrow on up to the hope that there is a time of peace and of more justice and brotherhood ahead. But we do ask what is the basis of a generally hopeful outlook, of what we call optimism with regard to the future. And the answer that modern man gives in the main is found in the idea of general or universal progress. Now what does that mean?

It means that life as a whole, and particularly human life, is thought of as a general or universal process, a movement upward from a lower to a higher level, whatever the criterion of this "lower" and "higher" may be. All too few, however, are aware of the fact that this idea of universal progress is a comparatively new idea. We can give almost the exact date when this comparatively new idea first appeared. It was only two hundred years ago, in the first half of the eighteenth century, and it was in France, that men first spoke of universal progress. It is, characteristically enough, in the period that we call the Age of Reason or the Enlightenment that this concept which since that time has become so widely accepted and so tremendously influential was formed. This period, the eighteenth century, was characterized by two closely related features, the high valuation of reason and a highly optimistic general outlook. The two are connected by the conviction that the specific nature of man, namely, his capacity to think or to reason, is capable of being indefinitely perfected. "*La perfectibilité de la raison*" (the perfectibility of reasoning) is a phrase of Rousseau's expressing not only a fact which indeed is, to a certain degree, observable both in the life of the individual and of humanity as a whole, but also the conviction that this increase in the power of reasoning and the knowledge gained thereby and in improved methods of applying knowledge must have unambiguously and unquestionably good results in the general conditions of human life. It is the conviction that if man can be educated to be more and more rational, more and more intelligent, it must lead to progress. Because man's knowledge grows and his capacity for applying knowledge increases, life must become better and better. This, in a nutshell, is the whole philosophy of progress. This idea of progress is based particularly upon science as the method of acquiring knowledge and technology as the method of applying knowledge, upon education as the method of increasing, accumulating, and transmitting knowledge, and upon organization as the method of combining the efforts of individuals.

However, in the nineteenth century Darwin's theory of evolution seemed so to support and enlarge this optimistic evaluation of progress as to see it in a cosmic perspective. Human progress seemed to be merely a special case of a general law of the cosmic process in time and evolution to be a process in which higher forms of life are produced, the highest of which is man, who, in his turn, continues this universal process by developing his specific nature, his intellect or reason, and thereby moving from lower to higher levels in the course of the centuries. The link between subhuman and human life was seen in the transition from primitive to civilized society, and progress, therefore, was seen primarily as a process of increasing civilization.

Although this idea of progress had a success for which the word "triumph" is hardly an exaggeration, there were warning voices raised against it, voices of men of weight and importance who were not willing to accept the new doctrine. It was a new doctrine because it was not known to antiquity, it was not known in the time of the Reformation, it was unknown in all Asiatic culture. It was a new thing! The idea of progress became an axiomatic conviction which needed no proof and could not be disproved. The belief in progress became, during the nineteenth century, a quasi-religious or pseudo-religious creed which to negate was a kind of blasphemy and a sign of malice, of distrust in humanity. Optimism was based on the idea of progress, and this was the religion in the later nineteenth century of those who had ceased to believe in God.

While the arguments of the opponents – to whom significantly belonged some of the greatest historians of the age like Leopold von Ranke and Jacob Burkhardt – were unable to shake this optimist progressivism and progressivist optimism, it was history itself that shook it to the very foundations. It was, first, the two World

Wars, with their unheard-of brutality and destruction; it was, second, the totalitarian revolutions and the formation of totalitarian states, with their appalling cruelties and their suppression of freedom; it was, third and most devastating of all, the discovery of the way to use the immense forces of the atom and their use as a means of warfare in atomic bombs, perfected in H-bombs, which exploded not only themselves but also that idea of progress. Since Hiroshima the world does not believe in progress any more. Totalitarianism has proved that organization as such is no guarantee that society will become more human. The most highly organized society has proved to be the most inhuman. The A- and the H-bombs have proved that the progress of science and technology is at least ambiguous. The tremendous increase in control of natural forces may be used for destructive as well as for constructive purposes. It has become evident that the basic error of the idea of universal progress lies in the fact that progress in knowledge is not accompanied by a corresponding progress of moral forces. As to these, no progress is visible. Therefore, we are faced with this situation; man, by his science and technology, now commands powers infinitely greater than those which were at his command in previous ages. But what use does he make of these powers? Is it a good use or a bad use? It can lead to the destruction of all human life, or it can lead to something good.

The optimism of the nineteenth century was based on a false assumption. Seeing that in the Western world there had indeed been since Roman times moral progress, a progress created by Christianity, men took progress in morality to be something inherent in human nature, not realizing that this progress was due to the Christian religion, which itself was a product neither of human nature or of the progress of civilization. It was only the experience of totalitarian brutality that revealed the true origin of Christian ethical standards as being in the Christian religion. This is particularly true of Europe. I would not object to giving the doctor of theology degree posthumously to Adolf Hitler, because he has done more than anybody else to awaken Europe to the consciousness of its Christian heritage by creating a world without Christianity. Where this Christian origin of Christian ethics faded out, where the Christian religion was waning, Christian ethical standards, which were derived from it, also decayed. Atheism, which became more or less the philosophy of the modern age, produced a quite different type of thought and behavior and ultimately led to the terrors of totalitarianism. Let me take this opportunity to say to the American people that if we and if you continue on the road of secularism, which means atheism, as we have during the past fifty years, we will surely end with totalitarianism. This is proved by history; it can be proved by philosophy.

The agnostic philosophy of the nineteenth century was not capable of reproducing the moral forces by which it had lived and which it had taken for granted.

This was the great illusion of the eighteenth and

nineteenth centuries – that we can have Christian morality without having Christian faith. Now that is gone. With the passing of this illusion the whole philosophy of progress broke down. In Europe the very word "progress" has almost disappeared from the language of the nations; nobody speaks of progress any more because nobody believes in progress any more. But America still has the ghost of progressivist optimism hovering about because America has had neither the experience of two World Wars on its own soil nor that of a totalitarian regime. But it is only a question of years – of a few years I should say – when this religion of progress will die out even in America. But if this hope of two centuries goes, what hope will then remain?

At this point we need to be reminded of a fact in our spiritual history that has not yet been mentioned. The idea of progress, we have said, is not a Christian idea. No New Testament writer, no medieval writer, no writer of the Reformation had any idea of progress. It is, as I have said, a rationalization and secularization of the Christian hope. It was by Christianity that mankind was taught to hope, that is, to look to the future for the realization of the true meaning of life. The peoples of Asia, the peoples of the pre-Christian world never looked to the future with hope, that is, with the expectation that it would bring realization of the true meaning of life. These religions are all ahistorical or nonhistorical in a double sense: they are not based on a historical fact or revelation as is Christianity, and they do not look forward to a goal of history as the full realization of its meaning.

This, for the first time, was given to the people of Israel; they looked into the future. Their religion, also, is based on historical facts. The religion of Israel is related to its history. Yahweh, the Creator-God, the Lord, has revealed himself in historical events which were seen or heard as the word of God by the interpretation of the prophets. At the same time it is these prophets who point to the future, from whence the definitive revelation, the Messianic Kingdom, is to be expected. This is the new thing in world history. The last of these prophets pointing to the coming Messiah was John the Baptist.

How concretely personalistic and historical his expectation was becomes apparent in the question that his disciples were sent to ask Jesus: Are you he who is to come, or shall we look for another? The answer that Jesus gave was indirect but it meant, Yes, can you not see from my works that I am indeed the one even though I am not quite what you anticipated? And again, in that great hour at Caesarea Phillipi when Jesus for the first time asked his disciples, "Who do you say that I am?" and Peter answered, "You are the Christ, the Son of the living God," Jesus accepted Peter's confession, declaring that it was not given him by human insight, by flesh and blood, but by God's own revelation. Jesus is the Christ, the expected One. The long looked for final revelation *has* come.

Now this, at first sight, seems to contradict what we said a moment ago, that it was by Christianity that mankind was taught to look to the future for the full revelation of the meaning of history. Indeed, the first thing to be said about the Christian faith, as was pointed out in the first lecture, is that it is based upon a fact of the past. It is exactly this which distinguishes the Christian faith from that of the Jew. The Jew still expects the Messiah, looking into the future for his coming; the Christian, looking back, says, "He has come."

Therefore Christianity seems to be a backward-looking religion, looking to the past, to the fact of redemption which has happened, once and for all. The Jews, not the Christians, seem to be the forward-looking people. But this is not so. Christianity adds to the basic word "faith" another equally basic word, "hope." How faith and hope, how the dimension of the past and the dimension of the future, are related in Christian doctrine is the main problem of this lecture.

First we repeat: faith is based on the past fact of the full and final revelation of God, which is at the same time the fact of redemption through reconciliation in the cross of Christ. This, indeed, is for the Christian the turning point of history, of world history which divides the whole of the history of mankind into two parts, B.C. and A.D., and this is the fact on which every Christian believer stands. However, this decisive change in the situation of mankind and of every individual, this victory of God's Kingdom over the powers of darkness, has a very strange form. This Messiah is a man hanging on a cross; he is crucified as a rebel. It looks like defeat rather than victory. But faith understands this paradoxical language of God. It is because man is such as he is, namely, a sinner, that Christ is as he is, namely, crucified, the Suffering Servant of God. It is because God's love is love-in-spite-of-us, love for the sinner, that it has to take this form. This was a scandal for the Jews. As we read in the first chapter of First Corinthians, the cross of Christ was a scandal for the Jews because they did not in the true sense recognize themselves as sinners. They wanted to be justified by their own works, that is, by themselves, not by grace alone. Christians understand that they have to identify themselves with this crucified Rebel before they can be identified with the risen Lord in his eternal glory. This double identification with Christ is faith. But faith alone is not all; faith is the origin of hope.

Christ, the crucified one, is, indeed, the Son of God, the Messiah. But this form of servant is not his real form made manifest. It is, so to speak, a disguise. The glory of God *is* manifest to the believer in the cross, but paradoxically; but the glory of God must still be manifested without paradox, directly. That is to say, Christ must appear in his true, unambiguous glory;

faith must become sight. Good Friday is D-day, but Easter is V-day; and for mankind Easter, V-day, means final glory. The Servant of God must appear in his true form; the King-Messiah must be no more hidden and the king no more a servant but a real king. Therefore Christ is not only the object of our faith as the Crucified One; he is also the object of our hope as the Glorified One.

This, then, is the content of the Christian hope. This is the Christian hope – not a part of it, nor an aspect of it; not a questionable form of it, but the Christian hope in its entirety, in its fullness. There should not be, as there has been, before, at, and after Evanston, any debate whether this might be a legitimate expression of Christian hope. This *is* the Christian hope, and there is no other. We should not worry so much about certain narrow-minded literalistic interpretations of the so-called Second Coming of Christ. We should not even worry about certain mythological expressions which we find in the New Testament itself. We should take the thing and not the words. Indeed, the forms of expression which the New Testament uses to tell us of the great thing yet to be expected, these are, as Bultmann would say, to be "demythologized" by, as he would also say, existential interpretation. Here the layman may close his ears; these are terrible words! But this is the topic of present-day discussion in Europe. There is something to be said for this proposal; we cannot live with the mythological forms of the Christian tradition or even with the letter of the New

Testament. What matters, however, is that we look into the future for the fullness of the coming of Christ.

We may not yet be able to produce an adequate eschatology, or Christian doctrine about the future fulfillment. I have made a small attempt in this direction in my recent book *Eternal Hope.* But this must be clear: The Christian faith produced with necessity the Christian hope, and the content of this hope is what Christ does to our future. You remember the program outlined in the first lecture: man lives in three dimensions, and for the Christian the question is, How does Christ affect my past, my future, and my present? We are now dealing with the second, How does Christ affect the future in my life? The topic of Evanston was the right topic and a good one, "Christ the Hope of the World," and that means Christ's ultimate, direct, and manifest victory, the fulfillment of God's world purpose which is announced in the cross of Jesus Christ.

If I am not entirely wrong about Evanston, there was behind the opposition to this eschatology of the ultimate hope a form of belief which is still very much in the blood and bone of American Christians, namely, the eighteenth and nineteenth century belief in progress. That was the belief and the hope which they wanted expressed at Evanston and Evanston was right not to give in on this point. If you believe in progress, you do it on your responsibility, but not as Christians. A Christian may believe, may hope that there will not be another World War. Such is also my hope. We may hope that there will be more justice than there is at present. We may believe or hope that there will be more brotherhood in the future than there is now. But we have no certainty in such hopes because they cannot be derived from the revelation in Jesus Christ. They are derived from the idea of progress, but this idea of progress is a thing of the past. In this Christians are behind the times; they still hold to the belief in progress which the world has abandoned, but they have no business to hold this belief as Christians. Such hopes, present hopes, optimistic hopes may be quite legitimate, but we have no Christian guarantee for them. Nobody can say that because Jesus Christ was here progress will occur. Therefore it is not our business to say that it will. On this point we have no certainty, and Christian hope is only that hope for which we have certainty in Jesus Christ himself. You may have certainty in regard to your belief in progress, but as soon as progress becomes doubtful to you, then this certainty vanishes. Now let me say something friendly about progress.

There *is* a form of progress, or of the idea of progress, that comes from true Christian faith, namely, that expressed in hope for the growth of the Kingdom of God within history. The apostles hope that the *Ekklesia* – falsely translated "the Church" – will increase, just as they hope that the individual will grow in faith, in knowledge, and in love. They hope that the gospel will find open doors rather than closed ones; they hope that through Christians the life around them will be influenced increasingly. However, they know that evil forces will also flourish with the passage of time. So they are not optimists. There is no optimism in the New Testament; optimism is a mark of the eighteenth and nineteenth centuries. *The* hope is the one which we can affirm with certainty because of Christ; this is the Christian hope. Other things we cannot affirm with certainty. We cannot say, They will occur because Christ has come. Yes, there will be growth in the Kingdom of God or of the Kingdom of God, but also there may be increase in the forces of evil.

Now the hope of the Christian is, as we have said, for the future perfection of God's Kingdom in the reign of glory, in eternal life, and in the eternal Kingdom. The hope of the Christian, therefore, is both personal and universal. The New Testament uses two terms, equally important but not quite identical, "eternal life" and "Kingdom of God," and this by necessity. The love of God is of all things the most personal; it is also the most universal. God loves me in Christ; but also God loves the world in Christ. To trust, to believe in, God through Christ is the most personal act we can perform. There is no act so personal as the act of believing in Christ, as identifying oneself with Christ. But to enter into fellowship or communion with God means to enter into the world enterprise of God, his world purpose, his Kingdom. The love of God which we receive by faith makes us world-minded, gives us a world outlook.

When we read the letters of the apostles we find them full of this world-wide perspective. A Christian cannot lead a merely private life; he is committed to the work of God in the world; he takes part in God's world plan. He is not concerned primarily about his own personal salvation; he is concerned about God's concern, which is for the world. His hope therefore must be both personal and universal.

Let us speak first about the personal aspect of that which the New Testament calls eternal life. I hope that you will not be shocked when I say that there is no personal immortality in the New Testament. The idea of personal immortality or the immortality of the soul is a Platonic and not a New Testament idea. Immortality, in the Bible, is an attribute of God. God alone is immortal, not the human soul. Eternal life has its origin, not in the indestructible nature of the soul, as in Platonism, but in God's gift and in his act of resurrection. Eternal life is not that which I have but that which God gives. And this eternal life which God gives is personal, not impersonal, just as the whole revelation in Christ is personal and not impersonal. Mystical religion and philosophical religion have no personal revealer and therefore no personal hope. Their hope is for unity with the infinite, and the common imagery is that of the drop of water in the ocean. That is their hope, to merge into the infinite as a drop of water is lost in the boundless sea. But that is not the Christian hope. We do not hope to be merged in the infinite like a drop of water in the ocean; the Christian faith does not hope for union; it hopes for communion. Here are two absolutely different and mutually exclusive systems. Christianity is the system of communion; Indian philosophy and idealism are a system of union or unity. You can have either the one or the other; you cannot have both. The God who speaks to us personally in love will not cease speaking to us in love for all eternity. And that gives us eternal life. The One who has revealed himself supremely in a person cannot allow us to be submerged in an impersonal eternity. Communion, I repeat, not union – God and man face to face – that is the picture the Bible gives of eternal life.

Now we must ask, Is this true, is it certain, can we be positive about it? Or are these just matters of speculation? I have found, to my great astonishment, many Christian leaders who are completely agnostic in regard to eternal life. They say, as does the world, "About such matters we do not know anything." The New Testament speaks a different language. Saint Paul says explicitly that we know. It is not a vague or arbitrary hypothesis; we know because of Christ. We know that nothing, not even death, can separate us from the love of God which is in Christ. And that is exactly what eternal, life is. Or, to put it in the words of Saint John, "he who believes in me, though he die, yet shall he live." To the agnostics – I mean the Christian agnostics – we can say what Saint

Paul said to the Corinthians: If there is no resurrection, then your faith in Christ is an illusion. Christ is either the guarantee of eternal life or he is nothing at all and the Christian faith is a tragicomic misunderstanding. Faith in Christ and hope in Christ are inseparable. The love of God in Christ is exactly that love from which nothing, not even death, can separate us. Therefore it is the basis of life eternal.

Now we may say that we cannot prove this any more than we can prove God's love. There is something, however, that we can prove and that is what the consequences are of the loss of this hope. If death is, really, the end of life, then the end of life is nothingness. Then life itself is devoid of meaning. If nothingness is the end, whatever comes before it is just a preface to that end which means nothing. If life ends with nothing, then it is nothing. As people are not willing to face this conclusion, they try to realize the meaning of life within time. Because they do not believe in eternity, they must have the purpose of life realized in time. And that is precisely what we call utopianism. Now utopianism seems to be a kind of friendly illusion; but it is, in truth, a terrible thing. Utopianism is the result of the panic of the closed door. Someone has said that if people try to create paradise on earth they will actually be creating hell instead. And that is what has happened in our time. If man is so panic-stricken that he thinks paradise must come within this earthly life, he is bound to take recourse to coercion and violence to produce it. And that is what utopianism always leads to, as we see in its most important modern form, Marxist Communism. A paradise created by coercion and violence is exactly what the quoted dictum means: hell instead. But I would say that there is no closer approximation to hell than this Communist paradise.

On the other hand we can understand what hope in eternal life, if it is really a certainty based on the fact of Christ, does to us. We said in the beginning of this lecture that hope, fear, and anxiety are the modes of expectation of the future. Apart from Christ expectation of the future is a mixture of all three. We cannot cease to hope, but we are not sure of our hope; therefore we are in anxiety. We fear certain things; so there is fear along with hope and anxiety. It is particularly the certain expectation of death that kills all hopes. We fear death rightly as annihilation. "*Nihil*" is Latin; it means "nothing." Death means nothingness, dissolution in the most absolute sense. Still nobody is quite certain that there is nothing after death. Therefore the form of expectation of the future is anxiety, that is, uncertainty whether what is to come will be good or bad. This anxiety is overcome by faith in Christ because the uncertainty is overcome in Christ. Hope, certainty, firm expectation of eternal life takes its place. Luther has a good translation of John 16:33: "In the world you have anxiety. But be confident, I have overcome the world." That is the gist of the gospel. We, so far as we are concerned, have anxiety in the face of death; but Christ, in whom we believe, of whom we are certain, removes from us that which necessarily creates anxiety.

The philosopher Heidegger, perhaps the greatest thinker of our time, has made it clear that human life is a life unto death, *Sein zum Tode*. Death is not merely something that comes at the end of life; it is present in every moment of life. Life is "being unto death." So far as Heidegger's analysis goes it is correct; I do not think that it can be seriously challenged. That is what our life is apart from Christ. But the Christian by faith knows something else. In the eternal love which Christ reveals to me there is hope which is the certainty of eternal life. The God who speaks to me in love now will speak to me in love for eternity. That is enough. Therefore this is hope without anxiety, victorious hope without fear.

How about the active mode of anticipating the future? So far as death is concerned the most complete activist has to admit that there is nothing to be done about it. You cannot do a thing against death. Americans have made great improvements in medical science and are to be praised for it. But we should not fool ourselves. All that medical science can do is to delay for a little the coming of death – say, for ten or twenty years, perhaps for forty years. But death will come just the same. All the fuss that is made about discoveries in medicine, therefore, come to nothing because those discoveries do not change our situation essentially. Whether I die tomorrow or thirty years from now, what difference in that essential situation does it make? But they do show one thing, these great efforts to lengthen life and the tremendous fuss that is made about any medical discovery. They show that man indeed does not want to die. You may laugh at death now but it is nothing to be laughed at. It is a grim thing; to die is a grim thing. To die without Christ is a grim thing; it means – to be annihilated. Everything that was of value just goes; it is no more, it comes to nothing, it comes to an end. And if you know it beforehand, your whole life is under the cloud of nothingness. That is why men do not like to think about death. Americans have built a billion dollar industry to help them to forget about death, the entertainment industry. We have a good deal of it in Switzerland too. This is a tremendous effort on the part of man to forget about death. But it doesn't succeed. Man pays billions for nothing. He can only put death out of his mind for a time, but it returns and he knows again that he will die. And he also knows still that if that is true the whole of life is devoid of meaning. This is what the nihilistic literature of the day brings out into the open very clearly, very bluntly, but very sincerely. It says that life has no meaning whatever. If life ends with death, that is true; but if life ends with Christ, that is a different matter. All the activism of our Western civilization rests finally on this basis of despair.

The hope of eternal life, however, does not, as Marx charged, have the effect of an opiate. Because it is based on love it cannot but create love, and love is the activity of which we shall hear more in tomorrow's lecture. Here let me mention one very widespread misunderstanding. Many people, trained in the doctrine of progress, have the idea that it is only the belief in progress that can stimulate man to activity, especially to social activity. What nonsense! As though the people of the Reformation period were inactive because none of them had the idea of progress. That is one of the fairy tales of our age – that men need the idea of progress to make them active. What we really need to make us active is love, and if we have love we need no other stimulus. One thing becomes evident by reflection on the idea of progress and activity. In his belief in progress in whom does man believe? In himself, of course! For that reason the idea of progress is such a flattering idea; therefore an assault upon the idea is taken as an insult to man, who by the idea makes of himself a god. The future for which the Christian hopes is not made by man but by God. But man is called by Christ to share in God's work, to become a coworker with him for the Kingdom of God – and this call is sufficient to activate man's total effort.

This brings us to our last point, the social and universal aspect of the Christian hope. God's purpose is not only to save or to redeem the individual person. As I have said before, God's plan is a world plan, the perfection of his whole creation in the eternal Kingdom. God's love is not confined to the individual person. God loves the world. Love in itself is outgoing and universal. Therefore the promise in Christ, the goal that is opened to us by faith as the content of hope is world redemption, world salvation. Eternal life is merely the personal aspect of this greater hope, the greatest possible hope. We cannot imagine what that means. Our imagination is too limited by time and space to foresee what this end of history beyond the limits of time and space will be. This limitation and insufficiency of our imagination, however, has nothing to do with uncertainty. We know that it will be the realization of God's plan, that it will be both the personal and the universal realization of the reign of God, the reign of love. We know it by our faith in what God *has* done in Christ. This knowledge about the future is based on a fact, the fact of which we have spoken before. For those who do not believe in this fact all that we have said about hope may be a great illusion. But for those who do believe in that fact it is the good news of hope.

Love

We have seen, so far, that faith is a relation to God's act of revelation and redemption in the past and that hope is the expectation of what God will do in the future. Now we have to show that love is the way by which God changes our present.

At first sight it might seem artificial to relate love, which is an ethical attitude, to the problem of time, which seems to be an abstract philosophical question. As a first approach, therefore, to the understanding of our thesis let us use some other words, quite simple ones in fact. Faith has to do with the basis, the ground on which we stand. Hope is reaching out for something to come. Love is just being there and acting.

But before we proceed farther we must make clear what kind of love it is of which we speak. You are certainly aware of the confusing multiformity of love. There are so many different kinds of love or, as we might say, so many levels of love from the lowest to the highest.' When people speak of "making love" they do not mean the same thing as when they speak of "falling in love" or "being in love" with someone. Again, love of the child for the mother or of the mother for the child, love of one's country, love of nature or of music, loving one's neighbor as oneself – all these are not the same thing but representative of an immense variety. We might try – as has often been done to arrange these forms of love in a kind of hierarchy, an order of high and low, and accordingly speak of "higher" and "lower" forms of love. This has been done particularly by the Scholastic thinkers of the Middle Ages and is being done today by Roman Catholic theologians. At the bottom of this scale would be love for material things, sex, pleasure, etc. At the top would be love of God as the highest or supreme good. This conception has been widely accepted and has exerted a tremendous influence throughout the history of Western thought. But from the Biblical conceptions of God, man, and the world there are strong objections to be made to such an understanding of love.

In our time the great work, *Agape and Eros,* of Anders Nygren, the Swedish theologian now bishop of Lund, has made a contribution to our understanding of love which seems to me to come much closer to the Biblical idea, although it may not be the last word on the matter. Love in the New Testament, called "*agape,*" is not only different in degree from "*eros*" but different in quality and in principle.

To understand this difference we start, with Nygren,

from an analysis of *eros,* taking this concept in its deepest and widest sense as first developed by Plato in his famous dialogue, the "Symposium." *Eros* is known to us mainly in connection with the adjective "erotic," a word that has a much narrower sense in English than in German and is close to what we call "sex." But in Platonic terminology it means any form of love that is determined by value. According to Plato, *eros* is an attraction produced in the soul by the value of the "beloved," a sort of vacuum effect by which the soul is attracted by something that it lacks. We love by *eros* that which is lacking in ourselves. You might call this a process of completion, the filling of a vacuum in the soul. But the most important thing is this, that *eros* is always determined by the quality of the beloved. We love, by *eros,* because the object of our love has a certain character – attractive, beautiful, or lovable. *Eros,* by definition, is motivated love; we love "because of ...," and insofar *eros* is a kind of reasonable or rational behavior. It is quite natural, quite understandable, that we love that which is "worth" being loved. Whatever this "lovableness" may be, whether of a lower order or a higher order, is now irrelevant. *Eros* is always directed to something lovable, whatever may make it lovable, and is, therefore, motivated by the quality of the beloved.

Now, is there any other kind of love? Yes, the New Testament *agape* does not have this character at all. It is not love grounded in the value, in the lovableness of the beloved; it is not attraction by the value of the object; it is not completion, and therefore it is not motivated. Unmotivated love – this is the nature and the mystery, we might say the paradox, of *agape*. If we think of *eros* as a motion of the soul, the motion of being drawn to, of being attracted by; then *agape* is a movement in just the opposite direction. It is not a being attracted or filled by the value of the beloved, but it is a "going out to," a giving, not a getting, of value. It is not comparable to a vacuum effect, a suction, but rather like a spring, gushing forth. Indeed Luther, a very profound interpreter of love, uses exactly this figure of speech to describe it – *quellende Liebe,* love like a spring gushing out or coming forth. In *agape* I do not love "because" of the quality of the beloved. If I love you because you are so and so, I love you with *eros.* But if I love you in spite of your being so and so, my love is *agape*. Most of us do not like to be loved in spite of what we are. But this is the very essence of *agape,* and particularly of God's love. There is no apparent reason why I should love anyone in spite of his being what he is. Neither is it understandable why I should be intent upon giving rather than getting. But that is the character of *agape;* it is a love that does not seek to fill my own soul, but to fill you; to replenish your emptiness and not my own.

A particularly clear instance of this love is found in loving one's enemy, the example Jesus uses to show what love means. If you love those who love you, he says, that is not real love, *agape*. But if you love those whom you naturally would hate, that is evidence of real *agape*. In this case it is obvious that it is not the quality of the beloved that motivates love. *Agape,* here, is clearly love for someone, not because of what he is, but in spite of his being just that.

But if *agape* is unmotivated love, the question arises of necessity, What is its origin? The answer that the New Testament gives is that the origin of this paradoxical love is God. You *can* love so only because God makes you love, by his love. Therefore we have to speak of God's love in order to understand *agape*. Now God does not love because he feels a deficiency in himself that needs supplementation. There is no vacuum in God that can be filled by something we have that he does not possess. God is in need of nothing, he is perfect in himself, he has all in himself. If he loves, his love is not *eros* but *agape*. He loves because he wants to give not to get, he wants to share, to give of his own to those who lack, who have need of what he gives. His love is entirely unmotivated by any value outside himself. His love, therefore, is entirely spontaneous, motivated only by his will to give, to share, to communicate his own, an expression solely of his free will. He loves for no other reason than that he wants to love.

What we said about love for one's enemies becomes supremely clear in his *agape* to us. He loves us, the sinners, not because of us, but in spite of us. We, as sinners, are not lovable to him. We are rebels against his will; we are, as Saint Paul particularly points out, his enemies. The reason for his loving us is certainly not our lovableness. He loves us in spite of our being such as we are. His love for us is solely and completely love "in spite of," not love "because of." And that is what we mean by the words "mercy" and "grace." It is mercy because it is undeserved – love in spite of our enmity and sin. It is grace because it is entirely from his free will that the love comes.

But one more thing has to be added. Not only does God love us with *agape;* God is *agape.* This is the greatest and most mysterious word of the New Testament: "God is love." Although we have known it since Sunday school days, and although it has been said so many times that we are almost tired of hearing it, still it remains the great mystery of the New Testament message. The statement that God is *agape* is found only in the New Testament. There is no other book of religion in which God is called love. God's love is not just an *attitude*; it is not just an act of God, it is the very essence of God. *God is love.* God is will, and the direction of his will is outgoing, sharing, self-communicating. This is his nature and this is the mystery of God revealed in Jesus Christ. God is sharing, giving, self-communicating love. This is the meaning of creation – God wants to go out of himself in order to glorify himself in other beings; he wants creatures with whom he shares his own life. This is also the origin of revelation; God wants to share and communicate the mystery of his being to us his creatures in order to glorify himself in us. This is also the origin of redemption, because God wants to restore and perfect his creation. It is also the supreme content of his revelation. God reveals himself *as* love and he reveals his love as mercy and grace, thereby giving perfect expression of his love as *agape,* and to *agape* as his own being.

We can understand the difference between *eros* and *agape* by noting the opposite "directions" of these two kinds of love. *Eros* is "upward-going," to the higher value, to that which is richer in value than the one who has it. *Agape* moves downward to that which is lower in value and poorer, to that which is in need. God himself, having need of nothing, goes out and down to his creatures who need him. The perfection of this "down-going" movement is incarnation and redemption in the cross of Christ. That is why the cross is the perfect revelation of God as *agape.*

Having made clear the dual meaning of love as both *eros* and *agape,* and the radical difference between these two terms, we return now to our starting point and ask, What, then, is the relation of *agape* to our existence in time? We asked, Why is it that we say, *Agape,* love in Jesus Christ, is Christ in relation to our present? What has *agape* to do with out present? We begin by saying, God's being, in distinction from our temporal time-bound existence, is eternal Being. This means that God is above the time process, above the transitoriness of creaturely, temporal beings.

The time process is the passing of everything from the future, where it is not yet, through the present, where it now is, to the past, where it is no more. And this time stream is irreversible. This is characteristic of all creaturely existence, this passing from the future through the present into the past. We are carried away by this time stream, and the stream of time goes incessantly, invariably and without interruption. The movement of this stream is always from not yet to now to no more. This transitoriness of our existence is fraught with deep suffering, even though we are not conscious of it. If you look at a photograph from earlier days and the tears come into your eyes, why is it? It is the experience of the time stream; that which was is no more. The suffering may be understood as an experience of disruption. You remember it was said that we live in the future, in the past, and in the present. But the three are never together. Hence the suffering. The three dimensions, future, past, and present, are not interchangeable like the three dimensions of space. The dimensions of spatial reality are interchangeable; those of temporal reality are unchangeable. The time stream never goes the other way. It always goes from the future, through the present, to the past. God's eternal being, however, is above this time stream.

For God there is no future; for God there is no past. There is no disruption involved in these dimensions. God does not change; for him there is no past, there is no future. His eternity has, so to say, contracted all three dimensions into one; the future and the past are his eternal present. But this point in God's existence is not really or merely a point, for it is all-embracing; it comprehends the past and the future in his eternal present. "A thousand years," for him, "are as a watch in the night," say the psalm. He is as he was and as he ever will be. To him the past is present and the future is present. His being is eternal, infinite, all-comprehending presence – something we time-bound beings cannot understand or imagine. His present is just the opposite of ours. Our present is only a point, a thin line of intersection between past and future. Something which a moment ago was not yet there is already gone before we are aware of it. *So* distracted is our time, *so* punctual is our present. But God's present is all-embracing, not distracted into past and future, but "assembled," united, one.

Even our present, however, is not a mere mathematical point, as it seems to be when we think about it. If in thought we form a concept of our present, it is like a line without breadth and the future passes through that line into the past. In lived reality, however, there is more to our present because we already live in that which is not yet, the future, and we still live in that which is no more, the past. By memory and expectation, therefore, our present is extended in both directions, to the past and to the future.

On the other hand, the reality of our present is questionable because we cannot really enjoy the presence of the future and the past. Our future, present indeed by expectation, is darkened and made unenjoyable by the fact that we not only expect it, we also worry about it; we fear it and are anxious about it. It is because of the uncertainty that we are anxious. The only thing that we are certain about, as regards the future, is that we shall die. And it is this that we fear. However, as we have said before, because we do not know what it is to die fear has the character of uncertainty, and an uncertain fear is what we know as anxiety. Therefore our present, always having in it the expectation of a future that is clouded by coming death, is darkened by anxiety. That is why we cannot really enjoy our present. But not only is our future darkened; so also is our past. Our future is darkened by anxiety about what is coming, our past is darkened by the memory of our guilt. We remember, inasmuch as we are responsible beings, that we have failed in our responsibility. We have not done what we ought to have done. You perhaps feel as I do: I should like an evening to come in my life when I can say, I have done what I ought to have done. So far no such evening has come. And this feeling, which is always more or less present in us and of which we are more or less conscious, this double feeling about the future which is darkened by anxiety and the past which is darkened by remorse, robs us of the true enjoyment of the present.

However, these two points need some qualification, lest I be called a pessimist! You may say, and rightly, that we also expect enjoyable things, like children looking forward to Christmas or a holiday. And we all remain children. And also that we remember not only our guilt but also the pleasant things that lie in the past. However, true as this is, the only thing that is quite certain about the future is death, and this is not only something unpleasant; it means that our whole existence is endangered by nothingness. If we are really human beings and not "butterflies," we can never forget about the whole, the totality of our life. The more human we are, the more this final event of total annihilation darkens our expectation of the future. The same is true with regard to the past. The more human we are, the more we feel ourselves to be responsible persons and the more heavily our guilt weighs upon our memory of the past. Therefore the more human we are, the less we can enjoy our present. It is only the "butterflies" who can really enjoy their present, and they do it at the cost of their humanity. The enjoyment of our present which is more than a mere point is impaired by both memory and expectation to the point of being destroyed. We are not really present because our heart is caught, as it were, both in the past and in the future, and so we cannot "forget about it." Our heart is not wholly here; being caught in the past and in the future, we are not really present.

This fact of our lacking a present comes out most clearly in our relation to our fellow men. We ought to be present for them, that is, open to their need, free to be with them wholeheartedly. Our individual existence becomes human only in the measure that we are with our fellow men. An isolated existence is not human, because we are created, not to be isolated, self-sufficient individuals; we are created for fellowship. Therefore we can be truly human only in communion with our fellow men. And that is exactly what is lacking in us; we are never really present with our fellow men. We may be with them in the same room, but we are not really with them but only beside them. It is not a "being with" but rather a "being without." We are shut in, enclosed within ourselves, because we are "preoccupied" with our own past and our own future. We are not present for them, not open and free toward them, because our hearts are possessed by our own anxieties, our own fears, and our own remorse.

Perhaps we can see this more clearly if we think of the state of mind that we call "depression." The condition of a soul in the extreme form of depression is just this, that he cannot free himself from his past with its guilt and remorse. And he cannot disentangle himself from his worries, anxieties, and fears about the future. Therefore he has almost no present. It is as if he were not "here." He is "there" – in the past and in the future. He is isolated thereby from his fellow men, shut in within himself. He is "without" instead of "within" his fellow men.

This depressed state, however, is only a very extreme form of what is our "normal" condition. In a lesser degree we are all "depressed" because all of us are distracted in the same way. We see our own character in the depressed person, only there it is magnified. We also are not present, and for the same reason. Now this lack of presence is nothing else than lack of love. Being with or in real openness for the other one is love. Being shut up within ourselves is lovelessness, the absence of love. Real presence would be real love, the sharing of self with the other, the giving of ourselves, being "within" instead of "without" him. And the reason for this lack of presence or lack of love is that we are entangled, caught, in our future by worry and in our past by remorse.

Our question now is, How does Christ change this condition? The answer of the New Testament, confirmed by every Christian, is this: *(a)* Christ makes us free from our past by making us free from our guilt, and he does it by taking our guilt upon himself. He says what the lighthearted, the "butterflies," say, but of course with a wholly different meaning, Forget about it. He says: Forget about it because that is mine. I carry your past; I carry your guilt. Faith in Christ means that our past is buried in Christ under the cross. Our guilt is there; we are done with it; we have nothing more to do with it. That is justification by faith. That is what it means to believe in redemption and reconciliation in Christ. *(b)* Christ makes us free from our future by saying: I am your future, therefore you need not worry; your future is secure in God's will. Your future is eternal life with God and with all of God's people. *You* need not worry about your future; your anxiety and fear can go, must go! I am your future; your future is guaranteed in me.

Now, in doing this, in freeing us from our entanglement with the past and with the future, Christ bestows upon us God's love and God's forgiveness, his *agape*. God's love toward the sinner is revealed and given to use in the crucified Christ. God's love is the guarantee of our future. His love is eternal, and whom God loves he cares for eternally, so that nothing can separate us from his love – not even death. But by giving us God's love, Christ makes us loving. The one who receives God's *agape* is not only a beloved son of God but also himself a lover. God's fire sets our hearts aflame. We cannot be touched by the fire of God's love without ourselves being set afire with the same love. God not only makes us believe in his love; he shares his love with us, makes us to participate in it. And this love is, as we have seen, free, giving, outgoing love.

And to become a loving heart instead of a worried, self-centered heart means to become "present." The man who receives Christ in faith receives presence, because God's love is presence. By *agape* he now has become capable of being "with" his fellow men. Perhaps you did not understand what I said before about our lack of being with our fellow men, because you thought of your own Christian experience. But as real Christians we are present with our fellow men; we have real presence.

We have asked: If *agape* is unmotivated love, from whence does it come? and the answer was that it certainly cannot arise *in* us. What is in us must be motivated. In ourselves there is only the possibility of *eros*, not of *agape*. *Agape* comes to us as God's gift and, more, as God's gift of himself. As the First Epistle of John says, "he who abides in love abides in God." He shares in God's love. Therefore his love is of the same kind– spontaneous, unmotivated, giving.

* * *

To conclude, having distinguished among faith, hope, and love, let us take them together in their mutual relation and unity. And, first, what is the relation of faith and love? It is a very simple relation. Faith is the hand by which we receive love, the way in which we receive God's revelation. Faith is nothing other than the vessel into which God pours his love, and therefore nothing in itself. Faith is about love; love is not about faith. Faith is nothing in itself but the openness of our heart for God's love. Thus faith and love not only are inseparably related, but become one with each other. For while the opening of our hearts is brought about by a relation to a fact of history, the cross of Christ, the heart once opened for the love of God in Christ is no longer related to a fact of the past but to a living presence. The crucified Christ received into the heart is no more a thing of the past; he has become the living Christ, he is present in the heart. Christ died on the cross; yes, but he lives through the resurrection. We do not believe in a dead Christ, but we live by faith in a living Christ. And the living Christ is the one who *now* fills our hearts with himself, with the love of God which is now as it was and as it will be from eternity to eternity. Faith, therefore, finds its end in the real presence of the living Christ. He is our present; it is he also who gives us presence. They are the same thing; by Christ and in Christ we are present with our fellow men. It is Christ who makes us to be present with our fellow men; it is Christ who fills our hearts with love.

And what is the relation of faith and hope? We have now the love of God in Christ. We are now filled with love and are, therefore, loving creatures now. But although this is true, it is still not the whole truth. For we are still living in the flesh, in the body of sin and death. The new life is, so to speak, superimposed upon our old life. It is something like a photograph taken on a film that had already been exposed; one picture is superimposed upon the other. That is what Christ does; he superimposes his image upon our old Adam, and this new picture is the new man. We have the divine light, but we have it as in a dim lantern. Therefore the love of Christ in us is often obscured. This is true in some degree of us all so long as we live by faith and not by sight. Faith is a dim lantern, in the words of Paul a dark glass, which means the same thing. Therefore we know that there is something more to be expected beyond that which now is, a fuller revelation, a fuller incarnation of God, or, rather, a real life of resurrection beyond death, beyond history, beyond the flesh of this body of death. The eternal life and the eternal Kingdom of God which have only begun in us in the midst of sin, darkness, and death – this will come in the full brightness of day. This expectation of the full realization of God's will is our hope. This hope has the same content as faith, namely, Christ. But it is Christ in the fullness of divine glory, no longer in the form of a servant, a crucified Christ. Faith believes what hope expects. Hope expects what faith believes.

But both faith and hope have their real content in the love of God revealed in Christ. That is what they are about. Faith and hope are about God, about the God of love, about God's love. Therefore they are nothing in themselves; they are something only by their relation to love. That is why Saint Paul says that the greatest among them is love. Not the most important – they are equally important, as we have seen. But love is the real substance of faith and hope. We cannot say, God is faith; we cannot say, God is hope, but we can say, God is love. That is what God is, and that is what faith and hope are about. But love in itself is not a mere "relation to"; love, *agape,* is the thing itself. It is his presence, it is himself here and now in us. It is his being as our new being, his presence as our own present. Inasmuch as we have him, we have love, and inasmuch as we have love, *agape,* we have him and we are "present." This presence manifests itself in our relation to our fellow men, but also in the state of our own mind and heart. It is joy and peace as God's being is joy and peace. Peace and joy are what everyone craves. That is true of every human being. But it is also true of every human being that his craving is not satisfied. Peace and joy can come into our hearts only by Christ, by God's own presence in them. There is no peace, within ourselves or with our neighbors, apart from reconciliation in Christ, because only if we are at peace with God can we have real peace in ourselves and with our fellow men. And peace with God we can have only through his forgiveness, through his taking away the burden of our past in the cross of Christ. Peace is the realization of his presence as our presence.

And joy! Joy is the feeling we have when we really are ourselves. But we can be ourselves only by being what God has created us to be – truly human. What makes us truly human is not reason, as the Greeks said; nor is it genius, or talent, or power, or intellect. All these can be very inhuman. It is only love in the sense of *agape* that makes us truly human. It is not cultural creativity but this simplest and deepest thing, *agape,* which makes us truly human. Giving love, not desiring love – spontaneous, unmotivated, unconditional love. That is what makes man truly human. That is why only by having this love can we know real joy. The three are so closely connected as to be almost identical; joy, peace, and love – the three go together. They cannot be taken away from us by any circumstance, not even by death. And that is real presence. The one who is in God's love is at peace; he has joy, he has love, and he is truly present.

This is eternal life as experienced already in this temporal life. Its source and reality are in God's love as already given to faith, as expectation to be completed by hope, as a beginning of presence in our own love. God's being with us is shared by our being with our fellow men.

This, then, is the unity in diversity of faith, hope, and love.

Also in the Emil Brunner Library:

Eternal Hope

Describing his objective in writing *Eternal Hope*, Emil Brunner boldly claimed that 'a church that has nothing to teach concerning the future and the life of the world to come is bankrupt'. Half a century later, such a challenge might still be levied. Against this backdrop, Brunner offers a way forward that is conscious never to stray far from scripture, yet nevertheless pastorally sensitive. Indeed, one of the central tenets of his approach is that the Gospel offers no comfort to the individual that is not at the same time a promise for the future of humanity as a whole. He proceeds systematically through the promises and mysteries that the Christian faith holds surrounding death, while holding the hope of eternity as a constant goal.

A precursor to his more rigorous Dogmatics, and partly in preparation for the second assembly of the World Council of Churches in 1954, Eternal Hope was also written just a year after the tragic death of Brunner's son. It is therefore no surprise that he combines the vulnerability of his personal encounter with death, and a theological outlook that has universal implications.

Published 2023

Paperback ISBN: 978 0 227 17922 2
PDF ISBN: 978 0 227 17923 9
ePub ISBN: 978 0 227 17924 6